N. R.
O. Chem.

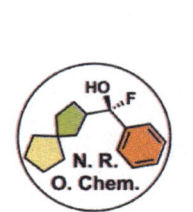

Named Reactions Handbook & Quiz

Practical handbook of +100 named reactions for advanced chemistry students and researchers

Volume 1

Lluís Llorens Palomo, PhD

www.nrochemistry.com

Copyright © 2023 Lluís Llorens Palomo
All rights reserved.

No part of this book may be reproduced, distributed or transmitted in any forms or by any means, including photocopying, recording or other electronic or mechanical methods, without the prior written permission of the author. For permission requests contact the author at lluis@nrochemistry.com.

Front cover by Julia Stefkova
Illustrations by Lluís Llorens Palomo created in ChemDraw

First edition, 2023.
Independently published
ISBN 9798854183536

Lluís Llorens Palomo - NROChemistry
Email: lluis@nrochemistry.com
Website: www.nrochemistry.com
Youtube: Named Reactions in Organic Chemistry
Instagram: Lluis_llorens_org_chem
LinkedIn: Lluís Llorens Palomo

Contents

Introduction 13

Part 1: 102 Named Reactions in Alphabetical Order 15

#1 Aldol Reaction 16
#2 Appel Reaction 16
#3 Arndt–Eistert Homologation 17
#4 Babler–Dauben Oxidation 17
#5 Baeyer–Villiger Oxidation 18
#6 Barbier Coupling 18
#7 Barton–McCombie Reaction 19
#8 Baylis–Hillman Reaction 19
#9 Birch Reduction 20
#10 Bischler–Napieralski Reaction 20
#11 Buchwald–Hartwig Coupling 21
#12 Chan–Lam Coupling 21
#13 Chugaev Elimination 22
#14 Claisen Condensation 22
#15 Claisen Rearrangement 23
#16 Clemmensen Reduction 23
#17 Cope Elimination 24
#18 Cope Rearrangement 24
#19 Corey–Bakshi–Shibata Reduction 25

#20 Corey–Chaykovsky Cyclopropanation 25
#21 Corey–Chaykovsky Epoxidation 26
#22 Corey–Fuchs Homologation 26
#23 Corey–Gilman–Ganem Oxidation 27
#24 Corey–Kim Oxidation 27
#25 Corey–Winter Olefination 28
#26 Criegee Oxidation 28
#27 Curtius Rearrangement 29
#28 Dieckmann Condensation 29
#29 Diels–Alder Reaction 30
#30 Eschenmoser–Claisen Rearrangement 30
#31 Eschweiler–Clarke Reaction 31
#32 Evans–Tishchenko Reaction 31
#33 Favorskii Rearrangement 32
#34 Fischer Esterification 32
#35 Fleming–Tamao Oxidation 33
#36 Friedel–Crafts Reactions 33
#37 Gabriel Synthesis 34
#38 Grieco Elimination 35
#39 Haloform Reaction 35
#40 Heck Coupling 36
#41 Hell–Volhard–Zelinsky Reaction 36
#42 Hofmann Elimination 37
#43 Hofmann Rearrangement 37

#44 Hofmann–Löffler Cyclization	38
#45 Horner–Wadsworth–Emmons Reaction	38
#46 Ireland–Claisen Rearrangement	39
#47 Julia–Kocienski Olefination	39
#48 Krapcho Decarboxylation	40
#49 Kulinkovich Reaction	40
#50 Kulinkovich–Szymoniak Reaction	41
#51 Kumada Coupling	41
#52 Ley–Griffith Oxidation	42
#53 Mannich Reaction	42
#54 Matteson Epoxidation	43
#55 Matteson Homologation	43
#56 Michael Reaction	44
#57 Mitsunobu Reaction	44
#58 Mukaiyama–Hayashi β-Keto Acetal Synthesis	45
#59 Mukaiyama Hydration	45
#60 Nazarov Cyclization	46
#61 Negishi Coupling	46
#62 Nicholas Reaction	47
#63 Noyori Asymmetric Hydrogenation	47
#64 Nozaki–Hiyama–Kishi Reaction	48
#65 Overman Rearrangement	48
#66 Parikh–Doering Oxidation	49
#67 Pauson–Khand Reaction	49

#68 Peterson Olefination	50
#69 Pictet–Spengler Reaction	50
#70 Pinacol Rearrangement	51
#71 Pinner Reaction	51
#72 Pinnick Oxidation	52
#73 Prins Reaction	52
#74 Reformatsky Reaction	53
#75 Reimer–Tiemann Reaction	53
#76 Riley Oxidation	54
#77 Ritter Reaction	54
#78 Robinson Annulation	55
#79 Roush Allylation	55
#80 Rubottom Oxidation	56
#81 Saegusa–Ito Oxidation	57
#82 Sakurai Allylation	58
#83 Sandmeyer Reaction	58
#84 Seyferth–Gilbert Homologation	59
#85 Shapiro Olefination	60
#86 Shi Epoxidation	61
#87 Simmons–Smith Reaction	61
#88 Sonogashira Coupling	62
#89 Staudinger Reaction	62
#90 Still–Gennari Olefination	63
#91 Stille Coupling	63

#92 Stork Enamine Aldol Condensation — 64
#93 Strecker Synthesis — 64
#94 Suzuki Coupling — 65
#95 Swern Oxidation — 65
#96 Takai Olefination — 66
#97 Tebbe Olefination — 66
#98 Tsuji–Trost Allylation — 67
#99 Van Leusen Reaction — 67
#100 Vilsmeier–Haack Formylation — 68
#101 Wittig Olefination — 68
#102 Wolff–Kishner Reduction — 69

Part 2: Quiz — **71**

Afterword — **175**

List of correct answers from Part 2 — **180**

About the Author — **182**

Introduction

In chemistry, a few words hold the power to describe complex transformations. Named reactions save time and help chemists communicate clearly. The language of organic chemistry can be arduous; I myself struggled with it during my Ph.D. However, learning it is inevitable if you want to become a renowned chemist. The *Named Reactions Handbook & Quiz* will bring you closer to mastering the language of this beautiful science, making it your second mother tongue and a must-have resource for your studies.

This reference guide and practice book equips advanced students with essential knowledge, and it also serves as an indispensable tool for synthetic or medicinal chemists in industry and academia. Within these pages, you will encounter over 100 named reactions, drawn from the annals of total synthesis and drug development as published in esteemed peer-reviewed journals. The *Named Reactions Handbook & Quiz* provides a bridge between theory and the real-world application of exhilarating scientific breakthroughs.

The book contains a curated selection of the most significant and versatile named reactions in organic synthesis. Each page showcases one or two remarkable reactions, with the reaction name as a title accompanied by a subtitle that unveils the target molecule behind the chemical transformation. Each example is referenced, ensuring that you delve into the latest and most relevant advancements in the field.

Prepare yourself for an intellectual challenge when the named reactions titles are erased, and their schemes become a tantalizing puzzle. The second part of the book tests your comprehension and reinforces your understanding of named reactions. The solutions are provided at the end of the book.

I genuinely believe this book will empower you with the language of named reactions, allowing you to communicate concisely, navigate the vast landscape of organic chemistry, and embark on your own scientific endeavors with confidence.

Part 1:
102 Named Reactions in Alphabetical Order

#1 Aldol Reaction

For the synthesis of Liangshanone

LDA, THF
-78 °C, 20 min, 52%

Angew. Chem. Int. Ed. **2020**, *59*, 23609.

#2 Appel Reaction

For the synthesis of (+)-Stemofoline

CBr_4, PPh_3, DCM
0 °C, 30 min, 95%

Nat. Commun. **2020**, *11*, 5314. Open access.

#3 Arndt–Eistert Homologation

For the synthesis of Suberosanone

1. TMSCHN$_2$, THF/MeCN
0 °C to rt, 10 h, 70%

2. AgOBz, H$_2$O, dioxane
80 °C, 10 h, 72%

Chem. Commun. **2016**, *52*, 6565. Open access.

#4 Babler–Dauben Oxidation

For the synthesis of (−)-Retigeranic Acid A

PDC, Celite®
DCM, rt, 12 h

(86%, 2 steps)

Org. Lett. **2021**, *23*, 5092.

#5 Baeyer–Villiger Oxidation

For the synthesis of (+)-Maytenone

1. *m*-CPBA, TFA, DCM 0 to 20 °C, 12 h
2. K$_2$CO$_3$, MeOH, rt, 2 h
(89%, 2 steps)

Angew. Chem. Int. Ed. **2021**, 60, 14967.

#6 Barbier Coupling

For the synthesis of Bryostatin 8

Sn, THF, Et$_2$O, H$_2$O
rt, 2 days
(67%, overall yield)

Angew. Chem. Int. Ed. **2018**, 57, 942.

#7 Barton–McCombie Reaction

For the synthesis of (−)-Lepadiformine A

1. NaH, CS_2, MeI, THF, 0 °C to rt, 24 h, 91%
2. AIBN, n-Bu_3SnH, toluene, 90 °C, 4 h, 93%

Org. Lett. **2020**, *22*, 3313.

#8 Baylis–Hillman Reaction

For the synthesis of Norzoanthamine

P(n-Bu)$_3$, $CHCl_3$, 0 °C to rt, 4 h, 80%

Angew. Chem. Int. Ed. **2021**, *60*, 12807.

#9 Birch Reduction
For the synthesis of (+)-Undulifoline

Li, NH$_3$, *t*-BuOH
-78 °C, 5 h
(87%, overall yield)

Angew. Chem. Int. Ed. **2021**, *60*, 12392.

#10 Bischler–Napieralski Reaction
For the synthesis of (–)-Yohimbane

POCl$_3$, DCM, 50 °C, 4 h
***then* NaBH$_4$, MeOH, 0 °C**
(35%, overall yield)

Org. Lett. **2020**, *22*, 4568.

#11 Buchwald–Hartwig Coupling

For the synthesis of Chalaniline B

Reagents: H_2N-Ph (aniline), $Pd(PPh_3)_4$, Cs_2CO_3, PhMe, 100 °C, 16 h, 48%

J. Org. Chem. **2021**, *86*, 7773.

#12 Chan–Lam Coupling

For the synthesis of (−)-Gardmultimine A

Reagents: $Cu(OAc)_2$, DMAP, MeOH, 4Å MS, rt, 8 h, 60%

Org. Lett. **2020**, *22*, 2022.

#13 Chugaev Elimination

For the synthesis of (−)-Rhodomollanol A

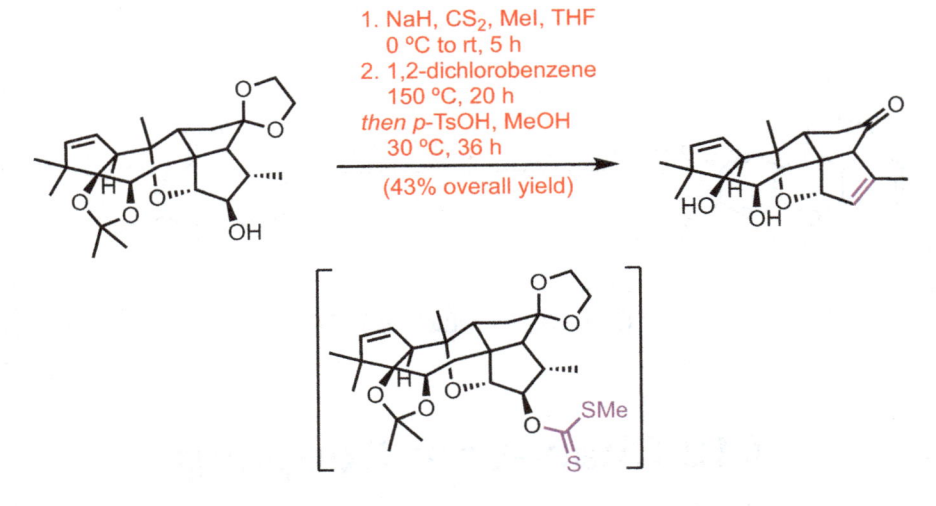

Reagents:
1. NaH, CS_2, MeI, THF
   0 °C to rt, 5 h
2. 1,2-dichlorobenzene
   150 °C, 20 h
   then p-TsOH, MeOH
   30 °C, 36 h

(43% overall yield)

J. Am. Chem. Soc. **2020**, *142*, 4592.

#14 Claisen Condensation

For the synthesis of (−)-Minovincine

Reagents: Cl-CH₂CH₂-CO_2Et, LDA, THF, −78 °C, 2 h

(75%, overall yield)

Angew. Chem. Int. Ed. **2020**, *59*, 13547. Open access.

#15 Claisen Rearrangement

For the synthesis of Curcusone A

DMF
140 - 150 °C, 18 h
(48%, 2 steps)

J. Am. Chem. Soc. **2021**, *143*, 4379.

#16 Clemmensen Reduction

For the synthesis of (−)-Hamigeran B

Zn powder, TMSCl
DCM/MeOH, rt, 2 h
≥ (72%, 99% ee)

Org. Lett. **2018**, *20*, 3687.

#17 Cope Elimination

For the synthesis of (±)-Phomoidride D

*m*CPBA, Al_2O_3
DCM, −78 °C, 10 min
(36%, overall yield)

Angew. Chem. Int. Ed. **2018**, *57*, 1991.

#18 Cope Rearrangement

For the synthesis of (−)-Vinigrol
(oxy-Cope reaction)

KH, 18-crown-6
THF, 0 °C, 2 h
then MeOH, −78 °C

97%, *dr* = 3.4:1

(3.4 : 1)

J. Am. Chem. Soc. **2019**, *141*, 3440.

#19 Corey–Bakshi–Shibata Reduction

For the synthesis of (–)-Conidiogenol

catecholborane
toluene, -78 °C, 24 h
90% (92% ee)

Angew. Chem. Int. Ed. **2020**, *59*, 16475.

#20 Corey–Chaykovsky Cyclopropanation

For the synthesis of (–)-Colchicine

NaH
DMSO, rt, 10 min
(53%, overall yield)

Org. Lett. **2021**, *23*, 2731.

#21 Corey–Chaykovsky Epoxidation

For the synthesis of (±)-Brussonol

Reagents: trimethylsulfonium iodide, ^{t}BuOK, DMSO, rt, 2 h, 88%

Org. Lett. **2019**, *21*, 6079.

#22 Corey–Fuchs Homologation

For the synthesis of Deoxypodophyllotoxin

1. CBr_4, PPh_3, DCM, 0 °C to rt, 16 h, 82%
2. *n*-BuLi, CO_2, THF, -78 °C to rt, 88%

J. Org. Chem. **2018**, *83*, 2018.

#23 Corey–Gilman–Ganem Oxidation

For the synthesis of (−)-Callophycoic Acid A

Reagents: NaCN, AcOH, MnO_2, MeOH, rt, 16 h, 97%

J. Org. Chem. **2020**, *85*, 3245.

#24 Corey–Kim Oxidation

For the synthesis of Protoilludane

Reagents: DMS, NCS, toluene, −20 – 0 °C, 2 h; then Et_3N, 0 °C to rt, 20 min, 95%

Angew. Chem. Int. Ed. **2017**, *129*, 9996.

#25 Corey–Winter Olefination

For the synthesis of Astellatol

Reagents: 1. Thiocarbonyldiimidazole, PhMe, 110 °C, 48 h; 2. P(OMe)$_3$, 110 °C, 48 h (74%, 2 steps)

Angew. Chem. Int. Ed. **2018**, *57*, 3386.

#26 Criegee Oxidation

For the synthesis of (−)-Conidiogenol

Reagents: Pb(OAc)$_4$, CH$_2$Cl$_2$, rt, 20 min (80%, overall yield)

Angew. Chem. Int. Ed. **2020**, *59*, 16475.

#27 Curtius Rearrangement

For the synthesis of Tetrodotoxin

Reagents: DPPA, Et$_3$N, toluene, reflux, 2.5 h; *then* allyl alcohol, DMAP, rt to 95 °C, 14 h, 75%.

Angew. Chem. Int. Ed. **2020**, *59*, 6253.

#28 Dieckmann Condensation

For the synthesis of (−)-Gardmultimine A

Reagents: NaH, MeOH, toluene, reflux, 21 h, 75%.

Org. Lett. **2020**, *22*, 2022.

#29 Diels–Alder Reaction

For the synthesis of (+)-Mannolide C

100 – 170 °C
2 h, 55%

Angew. Chem. Int. Ed. **2021**, 60, 21267.

#30 Eschenmoser–Claisen Rearrangement

For the synthesis of (±)-Clivonine

xylene, microwave
160 °C, 30 min, 81%

J. Org. Chem. **2020**, 85, 10035.

#31 Eschweiler–Clarke Reaction

For the synthesis of (−)-Nicotine

HCHO, HCOOH
80 °C, 18 h, 98%

Org. Lett. **2019**, *21*, 705. Open access.

#32 Evans–Tishchenko Reaction

For the synthesis of Bryostatin 8

SmI$_2$, THF
−10 °C to rt, 2 h, 90%

dr > 95:5

Angew. Chem. Int. Ed. **2018**, *57*, 942.

#33 Favorskii Rearrangement

For the synthesis of (+)-Perseanol

NaOMe, MeOH
55 °C, 4 h, 78%

Nature *573*, 563–567 (2019).

#34 Fischer Esterification

For the synthesis of Yicathin B

H_2SO_4, MeOH
reflux, 16 h, 45%

ChemMedChem **2020**, *15*, 749.

#35 Fleming–Tamao Oxidation

For the synthesis of (−)-Scabrolide A

Reagents: Hg(OAc)$_2$, AcOOH, AcOH, rt, 45 min, 55%

J. Am. Chem. Soc. **2020**, *142*, 8585.

#36 Friedel–Crafts Reactions

For the synthesis of Atlanticone C

Reagents: AlCl$_3$, DCM, 0 °C to rt, 10 h, 80%

Reagents: AlCl$_3$, 180 °C, 1.5 h, 87%

Angew. Chem. Int. Ed. **2019**, *58*, 14629. Open access.

#37 Gabriel Synthesis

For the synthesis of polycyclic compounds structurally similar to Amaryllidaceae alkaloids

1. Phthalimide, PBu_3, DIAD THF, rt, 1 h, 70%
2. N_2H_4, rt, 16 h, 51%

Chem. Eur. J. **2018**, *24*, 10069.

#38 Grieco Elimination

For the synthesis of Scabrolide A

J. Am. Chem. Soc. **2022**, *144*, 1528. Open access.

#39 Haloform Reaction

For the synthesis of Heliolactone

Org. Lett. **2019**, *21*, 4215.

#40 Heck Coupling

For the synthesis of Hinckdentine A

Reagents: CH$_2$=CH-CO$_2$Et, Pd(OAc)$_2$, NEt$_3$, MeCN, reflux, 81%

Starting material: 2,4-dibromo-6-iodoaniline → Product: ethyl (E)-3-(2-amino-3,5-dibromophenyl)acrylate

Org. Lett. **2021**, *23*, 2169.

#41 Hell–Volhard–Zelinsky Reaction

For the synthesis of Azabicycloheptane building blocks

Cyclobutanecarboxylic acid →
1. SOCl$_2$, reflux, 2 h
2. P, Br$_2$, reflux, 16 h
3. *n*-BuOH, 0 °C, 85%

Product: *n*-butyl 1-bromocyclobutanecarboxylate

Eur. J. Org. Chem. **2018**, *40*, 5596.

#42 Hofmann Elimination
For the synthesis of Pleosporol A

1. MeI, K_2CO_3, THF, rt, 20 h
2. DMSO, $(COCl)_2$, -78 °C, 30 min
   then TEA, DCM -78 °C to rt, 4 h

(81%, 2 steps)

Tetrahedron 81 (2021) 131913.

#43 Hofmann Rearrangement
For the synthesis of (–)-Ambiguine P

PIDA, KOH
H_2O, dioxane
rt, 20 h, 39%

PIDA
Phenyliodine(III) diacetate

J. Am. Chem. Soc. **2019**, *141*, 2233.

#44 Hofmann–Löffler Cyclization

For the synthesis of Nicotine

PhI(*mcba*)$_2$, I$_2$
DCM, rt, 16 h, 67%

PhI(*mcba*)$_2$

Org. Lett. **2019**, *21*, 705. Open access.

#45 Horner–Wadsworth–Emmons Reaction

For the synthesis of (−)-Gibberodione

K$_2$CO$_3$, THF, H$_2$O, rt, 2 h

(60%, overall yield)

J. Org. Chem. **2021**, *86*, 3074.

Named Reactions Handbook & Quiz

#46 Ireland–Claisen Rearrangement

For the synthesis of Clionastatin A

KHMDS, toluene
-78 °C, 30 min
then TMSCl
rt to 80 °C, 5 h, 80%

J. Am. Chem. Soc. **2021**, *143*, 13016.

#47 Julia–Kocienski Olefination

For the synthesis of A-94964

DBU, DCM, 0 °C, 3 h
61%, *Z/E* > 20:1

Angew. Chem. Int. Ed. **2022**, *61*, e202200818.

#48 Krapcho Decarboxylation

For the synthesis of (+)-Condyfoline

Reagents: KI, DMI:H_2O, 130 °C, 16 h, 93%

DMI
1,3-Dimethyl-2-imidazolidinone

Angew. Chem. Int. Ed. **2020**, *59*, 13990.

#49 Kulinkovich Reaction

For the synthesis of Bisdehydroneostemoninine

Reagents: ClTi(O*i*Pr)$_3$, EtMgBr, THF, 0 °C to rt, 36 h, 63%

Angew. Chem. Int. Ed. **2018**, *57*, 15209.

#50 Kulinkovich–Szymoniak Reaction

For the synthesis of AZD7624

Reagents: MeTi(O*i*Pr)$_3$, Et$_2$Zn, *i*PrOLi, LiI, 2-MeTHF, rt, 30 h, 37%

Org. Process Res. Dev. **2021**, *25*, 2351.

#51 Kumada Coupling

For the synthesis of Anthracimycin

Reagents: allyl-MgCl, PdCl$_2$(dppf), Et$_2$O, 0 °C to rt, 18 h (63%, overall yield)

Org. Lett. **2020**, *22*, 5550.

#52 Ley–Griffith Oxidation

For the synthesis of (−)-Flueggenines D and I

Reagents: TPAP, NMO, CH_2Cl_2, 23 °C, 20 h
(75%, overall yield)

TPAP — Tetrapropylammonium perruthenate

NMO — N-methylmorpholine N-oxide

Chem. Sci. **2020**, *11*, 10934. Open access.

#53 Mannich Reaction

For the synthesis of (±)-Tapentadol

Reagents: HCHO, $HN(CH_3)_2$ (dimethylamine), DMSO, rt, 24 h, 76%

Org. Process Res. Dev. **2019**, *23*, 1369.

#54 Matteson Epoxidation

For the synthesis of (–)-Cajanusine

*nBuLi, CH$_2$Br$_2$, THF
-78 °C to rt, 16 h, 65%*

J. Am. Chem. Soc. **2020**, *142*, 5002.

#55 Matteson Homologation

For the synthesis of (+)-Galbulin

CH$_2$ICl, *n*BuLi, THF
-78 °C to rt, 35 min
(51%, overall yield)

Org. Lett. **2020**, *22*, 6780.

#56 Michael Reaction

For the synthesis of Kopsinitarine E

K$_2$CO$_3$, acetone
rt, 40 h, 72%

Angew. Chem. Int. Ed. **2020**, *59*, 22039.

#57 Mitsunobu Reaction

For the synthesis of Curcusone A

DEAD, PPh$_3$, THF
0 to 50 °C, 30 min

(48%, overall yield)

J. Am. Chem. Soc. **2021**, *143*, 4379.

#58 Mukaiyama–Hayashi β-Keto Acetal Synthesis

For the synthesis of Curcusone A

TBSOTf, Et$_3$N, DCM
0 °C to rt, 25 min
then HC(OEt)$_3$
BF$_3$·OEt$_2$, 0 °C, 25 min

(73%, overall yield)

J. Am. Chem. Soc. **2021**, *143*, 4379.

#59 Mukaiyama Hydration

For the synthesis of Arcutine

Mn(acac)$_2$, PhSiH$_3$, O$_2$
EtOH, rt, 2.5 h, 81%

J. Am. Chem. Soc. **2019**, *141*, 13718.

#60 Nazarov Cyclization

For the synthesis of (−)-Himalensine A

Reagents: SnCl$_4$, DCM, 0 °C to rt, 30 min, 75%

Angew. Chem. Int. Ed. **2019**, *58*, 7390.

#61 Negishi Coupling

For the synthesis of (+)-Peniciketals A and B

Reagents: TMP, *n*-BuLi, THF; then ZnCl$_2$, Pd(PPh$_3$)$_4$, acryloyl chloride, −78 °C – rt, 16 h, 80%

LiTMP

Acryloyl chloride

J. Am. Chem. Soc. **2021**, *143*, 1740.

#62 Nicholas Reaction

For the synthesis of Halichondrin B

1. $Co_2(CO)_8$, DCM, rt, 1 h
2. $BF_3 \cdot Et_2O$, rt, 3.5 h
3. CAN, acetone, 0 °C to rt, 1 h

(72%, *dr* = 5:1, 3 steps)

J. Am. Chem. Soc. **2021**, *143*, 9267.

#63 Noyori Asymmetric Hydrogenation

For the synthesis of (−)-Talatisamine

H_2, 1100 psi
$RuCl_2[(R)\text{-BINAP}]$
EtOH, 30 °C, 6 days, 76%

ACS Cent. Sci. **2021**, *7*, 1311. Open access.

#64 Nozaki–Hiyama–Kishi Reaction

For the synthesis of (+)-Pepluanol A

Reagents: NiCl$_2$, CrCl$_2$, DMF, rt to 50 °C, 1 h, 63%

J. Am. Chem. Soc. **2021**, *143*, 11934.

#65 Overman Rearrangement

For the synthesis of (−)-Himeradine A

Reagents:
1. Cl$_3$CCN, DBU, DCM, 0 °C to rt, 2 h, 95%
2. *R*-(−)-COP-Cl, DCM, rt, 18 h, 85%

Angew. Chem. Int. Ed. **2019**, *58*, 16193.

#66 Parikh–Doering Oxidation

For the synthesis of Enterocin

Reagents: $SO_3 \cdot py$, $i\text{-}Pr_2NEt$, DMSO, DCM, 0 °C, 1 h, 84%

Angew. Chem. Int. Ed. **2021**, *60*, 20269. Open access.

#67 Pauson–Khand Reaction

For the synthesis of (+)-Waihoensene

Reagents: $Co_2(CO)_8$, CO, mesitylene, rt to 160 °C, 26 h, 50%

Angew. Chem. Int. Ed. **2020**, *59*, 13521.

#68 Peterson Olefination

For the synthesis of Bufospirostenin A

J. Am. Chem. Soc. **2020**, *142*, 12602.

#69 Pictet–Spengler Reaction

For the synthesis of (+)-Arborisidine

J. Am. Chem. Soc. **2019**, *141*, 7715.

#70 Pinacol Rearrangement

For the synthesis Kopsinitarine E
(semipinacol reaction)

Ag₂CO₃, toluene, 110 °C, 10 h, 86%

Angew. Chem. Int. Ed. **2020**, *59*, 22039.

#71 Pinner Reaction

For the synthesis of Dabigatran etexilate mesylate

*EtOH·HCl, 40 °C, 6 h
then NH₃, (NH₄)₂CO₃
30 °C, 10 h, 97%*

ACS Omega **2018**, *3*, 5744. Open access.

#72 Pinnick Oxidation

For the synthesis of Tetrodotoxin

NaClO$_2$, NaH$_2$PO$_4$
t-BuOH/H$_2$O, rt, 14 h, 71%

Angew. Chem. Int. Ed. **2020**, *59*, 6253.

#73 Prins Reaction

For the synthesis of Talatisamine

Hg(OAc)$_2$
AcOH, 60 °C, 1 h
(29%, overall yield)

Angew. Chem. Int. Ed. **2020**, *59*, 479.

#74 Reformatsky Reaction

For the synthesis of (−)-Artemisinin

Reagents: BrCH₂CO₂Et, Zn, toluene, 90 °C, 35 min, 86%

Angew. Chem. Int. Ed. **2018**, *57*, 8293.

#75 Reimer–Tiemann Reaction

For the synthesis of Ziziphine N

Reagents: $CHCl_3$, NaOH, H_2O, EtOH, 70 °C, 4 h, 41%

Org. Lett. **2007**, *9*, 1367.

#76 Riley Oxidation

For the synthesis of (−)-Mitrephorone A

SeO$_2$
1,4-dioxane
100 °C, 7 h, 70%

J. Am. Chem. Soc. **2019**, *141*, 19589.

#77 Ritter Reaction

For the synthesis of Hapalindole K

H$_2$SO$_4$, TMSCN
0 °C to rt, 1 h, 48%

Angew. Chem. Int. Ed. **2011**, *50*, 7641.

#78 Robinson Annulation

For the synthesis of (–)-Mitrephorones A and B

Reagents: methyl vinyl ketone; Et₃N, DCM, rt, 96 h *then* NaOMe, MeOH, rt, 24 h (57%, overall yield)

J. Am. Chem. Soc. **2019**, *141*, 19589.

#79 Roush Allylation

For the synthesis of Aplysiasecosterol A

Reagent: 2-bromoallyl boronate with (CO₂CH^{i}Pr₂) tartrate ester; toluene/pentane, –95 °C, 2 h, 88%

J. Am. Chem. Soc. **2018**, *140*, 9211.

#80 Rubottom Oxidation

For the synthesis of (−)-Conidiogenol

1. TMSOTf, Et$_3$N, DCM, 0 °C, 2.5 h
2. MeReO$_3$, H$_2$O$_2$, Py
   AcOH, MeCN, 0 °C to rt, 30 min
   then PPTS, rt, 2 h

(91%, *dr* ≥ 10:1, 2 steps)

Angew. Chem. Int. Ed. **2020**, *59*, 16475.

#81 Saegusa–Ito Oxidation

For the synthesis of (+)-Pepluanol A

1. LiTMP, TMSCl, THF
   -78 °C to rt, 40 min
2. allylmethylcarbonate
   $Pd_2(dba)_3$, MeCN
   40 °C, 3 h, 96%

J. Am. Chem. Soc. **2021**, *143*, 11934.

#82 Sakurai Allylation

For the synthesis of Laurendecumallene B

Reagents: allyl-TMS, TiCl$_4$, DCM, -78 °C to rt, 35 min, 89%

Chem. Sci. **2020**, *11*, 3036. Open access.

#83 Sandmeyer Reaction

For the synthesis of Ramelteon

Reagents: H$_2$SO$_4$, NaNO$_2$, H$_2$O then Et$_2$O, NaI, 0 °C to rt, 3.5 h, 70%

ChemCatChem **2019**, *11*, 5762.

#84 Seyferth–Gilbert Homologation

For the synthesis of (+)-Heilonine

J. Am. Chem. Soc. **2021**, *143,* 16394. Open access

#85 Shapiro Olefination

For the synthesis of (−)-Akaol A

1. NH$_2$NHTs, PPTS, THF, rt, 12 h
2. *n*-BuLi, THF, 0 °C to rt, 5 h, 60%

Org. Chem. Front. **2018**, *5*, 1886.

#86 Shi Epoxidation

For the synthesis of Euonyminol

Reagents: (−)-Shi catalyst, Oxone, K_2CO_3, MeCN, 0 °C to rt, 3 h, 70%

(−)-Shi catalyst

J. Am. Chem. Soc. **2021**, *143*, 699.

#87 Simmons–Smith Reaction

For the synthesis of Pre-schisanartanin C

Reagents: Et_2Zn, TFA, CH_2I_2, DCM, −10 °C – rt, 14 h, 90%

J. Am. Chem. Soc. **2020**, *142*, 573.

#88 Sonogashira Coupling

For the synthesis of Justicidone

Reagents: propargyl alcohol (HC≡C-CH$_2$OH), PdCl$_2$(PPh$_3$)$_2$, CuI, i-Pr$_2$NH, THF, rt, 3 h, 89%

Substrate: 5-iodo-1,3-benzodioxole → Product: 5-(3-hydroxyprop-1-yn-1-yl)-1,3-benzodioxole

Org. Lett. **2020**, *22*, 265.

#89 Staudinger Reaction

For the synthesis of (−)-Metaphanine

Conditions:
1. MsCl, TEA, DMF, 0 °C, 10 min then NaN$_3$, 0 to 65 °C, 6 h, 92%
2. PPh$_3$, H$_2$O, THF, rt to 65 °C, 6 h then Boc$_2$O, rt, 1 h, 90%

Starting material contains: Br, OTIPS, OMOM, OMe, OMe, HO
Intermediate (in brackets): azide (N$_3$) intermediate
Product: BocHN with Br, OTIPS, OMOM, OMe, OMe substituents

J. Am. Chem. Soc. **2021**, *143*, 2699.

#90 Still–Gennari Olefination

For the synthesis of (+)-Euphorikanin A

Reagents: (CF$_3$CH$_2$O)$_2$P(O)CH$_2$CO$_2$Me, 18-crown-6, KHMDS, THF, −78 °C, 3 h, 78%

J. Am. Chem. Soc. **2021**, *143*, 8261.

#91 Stille Coupling

For the synthesis of (+)-Ambiguine G

Reagents: CH$_2$=C(OEt)SnBu$_3$, Pd(dppf)Cl$_2$·DCM, CuI, LiCl, DMF, 40 °C, 2.5 days, 87%

J. Am. Chem. Soc. **2021**, *143*, 10872. Open access.

#92 Vinylogous Stork Enamine Aldol Condensation

For the synthesis of Anmindenol A

Bu$_2$BOTf, THF
rt, 3 h, (77%, *E/Z* = 7:1)

J. Org. Chem. **2019**, *84*, 10953.

#93 Strecker Synthesis

For the synthesis of (+)-Flavsiamine F

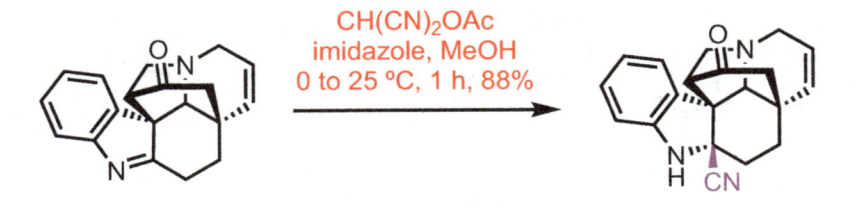

CH(CN)$_2$OAc
imidazole, MeOH
0 to 25 °C, 1 h, 88%

Angew. Chem. Int. Ed. **2019**, *58*, 5443.

#94 Suzuki Coupling

For the synthesis of (+)-Alstilobanine C

Reagents: 2-nitrophenylboronic acid, $Pd_2(dba)_3$, JohnPhos, Cs_2CO_3, THF/H_2O, 40 °C, 2.5 h, 90%

Angew. Chem. Int. Ed. **2021**, *60*, 12392.

#95 Swern Oxidation

For the synthesis of (+)-Condyfoline

Reagents: $(COCl)_2$, DMSO, NEt_3, DCM, −78 °C, 1 h, 84%

Angew. Chem. Int. Ed. **2020**, *59*, 13990.

#96 Takai Olefination

For the synthesis of Pre-schisanartanin C

Reagents: CrCl$_2$, CHI$_3$, THF, 0 °C to rt, 3 h, 84%

J. Am. Chem. Soc. **2020**, *142*, 573.

#97 Tebbe Olefination

For the synthesis of (–)-Dehydrocostus lactone

Reagents: Cp$_2$Ti(Cl)(AlMe$_2$), THF, 0 °C to rt, 30 min, 59%

Org. Lett. **2021**, *23*, 1344.

#98 Tsuji–Trost Allylation

For the synthesis of (+)-Condyfoline

Reagents: MeO$_2$C-CH$_2$-CO$_2$Me, Pd(PPh$_3$)$_4$, t-BuOK, THF, 0 to 50 °C, 12 h, 90%

Angew. Chem. Int. Ed. **2020**, *59*, 13990.

#99 Van Leusen Reaction

For the synthesis of (−)-Conidiogenol

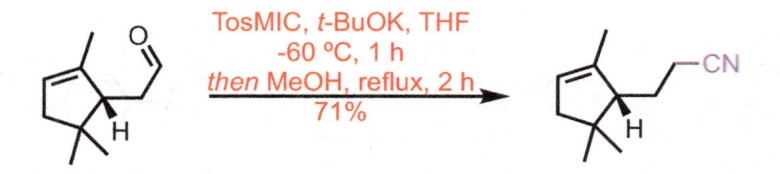

Reagents: TosMIC, t-BuOK, THF, −60 °C, 1 h; *then* MeOH, reflux, 2 h, 71%

Angew. Chem. Int. Ed. **2020**, *59*, 16475.

#100 Vilsmeier–Haack Formylation

For the synthesis of Lyconesidine B

Org. Lett. **2021**, *23*, 676.

#101 Wittig Olefination

For the synthesis of (+)-Haperforin G

J. Am. Chem. Soc. **2020**, *142*, 19487.

#102 Wolff–Kishner Reduction

For the synthesis of (+)-Maytenone

NH$_2$NH$_2$
KOH, DGME
rt to 194 °C, 5 h, 61%

Angew. Chem. Int. Ed. **2021**, *60*, 14967.

Part 2:
Quiz

#1

A	Noyori Asymmetric Hydrogenation
B	Staudinger Reaction
C	Corey–Bakshi–Shibata Reduction
D	Evans–Tishchenko Reaction

#2

NiCl₂, CrCl₂, DMF
rt to 50 °C, 1 h, 63%

A	Barbier Coupling
B	Nozaki–Hiyama–Kishi Reaction
C	Strecker Condensation
D	Grignard Reaction

#3

A	Hofmann Rearrangement
B	Overman Rearrangement
C	Pinacol Rearrangement
D	Curtius Rearrangement

#4

Cu(OAc)₂, DMAP, MeOH, 4Å MS, rt, 8 h, 60%

A	Buchwald–Hartwig Coupling
B	Ullmann Coupling
C	Suzuki Coupling
D	Chan–Lam Coupling

#5

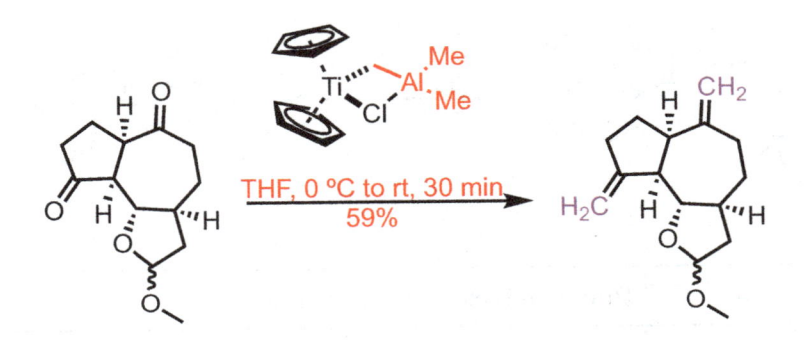

A	Kulinkovich Reaction
B	Wittig Olefination
C	Tebbe Olefination
D	Peterson Olefination

#6

TBSOTf, Et$_3$N, DCM
0 °C to rt, 25 min
then HC(OEt)$_3$
BF$_3$·OEt$_2$, 0 °C, 25 min

(73%, overall yield)

A	Mukaiyama–Hayashi β-Keto Acetal Synthesis
B	Aldol Reaction
C	Claisen Condensation
D	Robinson Annulation

#7

mCPBA, Al$_2$O$_3$
DCM, -78 °C, 10 min
(36%, overall yield)

A	Hofmann Elimination
B	Eschweiler–Clarke Reaction
C	Grieco Elimination
D	Cope Elimination

#8

A	Corey–Kim Oxidation
B	Rubottom Oxidation
C	Parikh–Doering Oxidation
D	Ley–Griffith Oxidation

#9

PDC, Celite®
DCM, rt, 12 h
(86%, 2 steps)

A	Corey–Kim Oxidation
B	Ley–Griffith Oxidation
C	Babler–Dauben Oxidation
D	Rubottom Oxidation

#10

KI, DMI:H₂O
130 °C, 16 h, 93%

DMI
1,3-Dimethyl-2-imidazolidinone

A	Krapcho Decarboxylation
B	Knoevenagel Condensation
C	Malonic Ester Synthesis
D	Grieco Elimination

#11

1. NaH, CS₂, MeI, THF
   0 °C to rt, 5 h
2. 1,2-dichlorobenzene
   150 °C, 20 h
   then p-TsOH, MeOH
   30 °C, 36 h

(43% overall yield)

A	Chugaev Elimination
B	Grieco Elimination
C	Barton–McCombie Reaction
D	Cope Elimination

#12

A	Kulinkovich Reaction
B	Negishi Coupling
C	Simmons–Smith Reaction
D	Skraup Reaction

#13

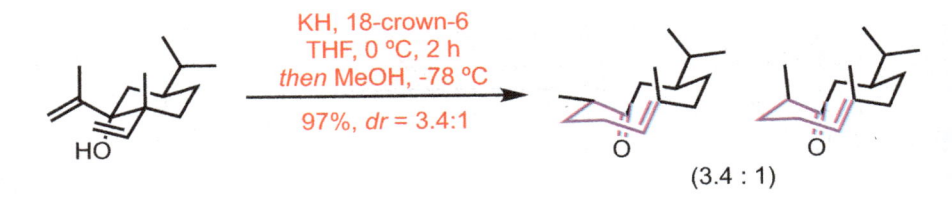

KH, 18-crown-6
THF, 0 °C, 2 h
then MeOH, -78 °C
97%, *dr* = 3.4:1

(3.4 : 1)

A	Hofmann Rearrangement
B	Cope Rearrangement
C	Beckmann Rearrangement
D	Claisen Rearrangement

#14

A	Tebbe Olefination
B	Wittig Olefination
C	Takai Olefination
D	Julia–Kocienski Olefination

#15

A	Bischler–Napieralski Reaction
B	Eschweiler–Clarke Reaction
C	Cope Elimination
D	Leuckart–Wallach Reaction

#16

Zn powder, TMSCl
DCM/MeOH, rt, 2 h
≥ (72%, 99% ee)

A	Clemmensen Reduction
B	Wolff–Kishner Reduction
C	Evans–Tishchenko Reaction
D	Staudinger Reaction

#17

A	Gattermann–Koch Reaction
B	Clemmensen Reaction
C	Barbier Coupling
D	Friedel–Crafts Reaction

#18

A	Simmons–Smith Reaction
B	Corey–Chaykovsky Cyclopropanation
C	Kulinkovich Reaction
D	Corey–Fuchs Homologation

#19

1. NH₂NHTs, PPTS, THF, rt, 12 h
2. *n*-BuLi, THF, 0 °C to rt, 5 h, 60%

A	Wolff–Kishner Reduction
B	Shapiro Olefination
C	Grieco Elimination
D	Corey–Winter Olefination

#20

A	Pinnick Oxidation
B	Pinner Reaction
C	Prins Reaction
D	Pinacol Rearrangement

#21

Et₃N, DCM, rt, 96 h
then NaOMe
MeOH, rt, 24 h

(57%, overall yield)

A	Claisen Condensation
B	Robinson Annulation
C	Dieckmann Condensation
D	Michael Reaction

#22

A	Appel Reaction
B	Mitsunobu Reaction
C	Staudinger Reaction
D	Nicholas Reaction

#23

A	Grignard Reaction
B	Negishi Coupling
C	Barbier Coupling
D	Kumada Coupling

#24

1. TMSCHN$_2$, THF/MeCN
   0 °C to rt, 10 h, 70%

2. AgOBz, H$_2$O, dioxane
   80 °C, 10 h, 72%

A	Arndt-Eistert Homologation
B	Doering–LaFlamme Reaction
C	Corey-Fuchs Homologation
D	Sandmeyer Reaction

#25

A	Sakurai Allylation
B	Grignard Reaction
C	Tsuji-Trost Allylation
D	Hiyama Coupling

#26

A	Michael Reaction
B	Mannich Reaction
C	Vinylogous Stork Enamine Aldol Condensation
D	Knoevenagel Condensation

#27

A	Corey–Gilman–Ganem Oxidation
B	Corey–Kim Oxidation
C	Ley–Griffith Oxidation
D	Swern Oxidation

#28

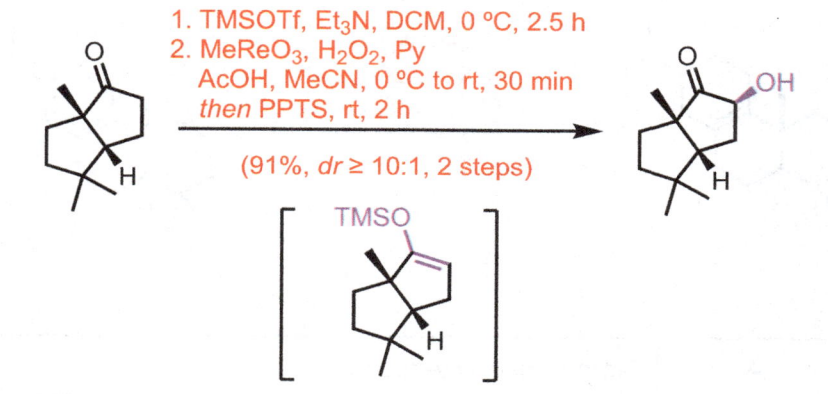

1. TMSOTf, Et₃N, DCM, 0 °C, 2.5 h
2. MeReO₃, H₂O₂, Py
   AcOH, MeCN, 0 °C to rt, 30 min
   then PPTS, rt, 2 h

(91%, *dr* ≥ 10:1, 2 steps)

A	Saegusa-Ito Oxidation
B	Wacker Oxidation
C	Rubottom Oxidation
D	Babler-Dauben Oxidation

#29

NH₂NH₂
KOH, DGME
rt to 194 °C, 5 h, 61%

A	Clemmensen Reduction
B	Birch Reduction
C	Wolff–Kishner Reduction
D	Shapiro Reaction

#30

A	Negishi Coupling
B	Grignard Reaction
C	Barbier Coupling
D	Kumada Coupling

#31

A	Mitsunobu Reaction
B	Staudinger Reaction
C	Appel Reaction
D	Haloform Reaction

#32

A	Chugaev Elimination
B	Grieco Elimination
C	Hofmann Elimination
D	Peterson Olefination

#33

H₂SO₄, NaNO₂, H₂O
then Et₂O, NaI
0 °C to rt, 3.5 h, 70%

A	Balz–Schiemann Reaction
B	Finkelstein Reaction
C	Sandmeyer Reaction
D	Haloform Reaction

Named Reactions Handbook & Quiz

#34

SeO₂
1,4-dioxane
100 °C, 7 h, 70%

A	Wacker Oxidation
B	Rubottom Oxidation
C	Criegee Oxidation
D	Riley Oxidation

#35

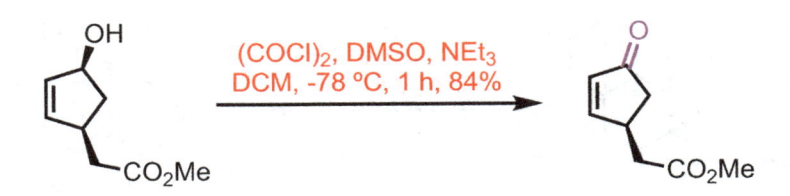

(COCl)$_2$, DMSO, NEt$_3$, DCM, -78 °C, 1 h, 84%

A	Corey–Kim Oxidation
B	Swern Oxidation
C	Ley–Griffith Oxidation
D	Parikh–Doering Oxidation

#36

DMF
140 - 150 °C, 18 h
(48%, 2 steps)

A	Cope Rearrangement
B	Curtius Rearrangement
C	Claisen Rearrangement
D	Oxy-Cope Rearrangement

#37

1. SOCl$_2$, reflux, 2 h
2. P, Br$_2$, reflux, 16 h
3. n-BuOH, 0 °C, 85%

A	Reformatsky Reaction
B	Hell–Volhard–Zelinsky Reaction
C	Haloform Reaction
D	Mitsunobu Reaction

#38

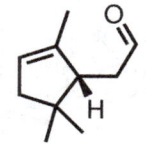

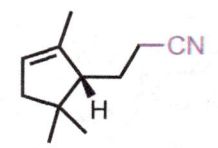

A	Matteson Reaction
B	Seyferth–Gilbert Homologation
C	Arndt–Eistert Homologation
D	Van Leusen Reaction

#39

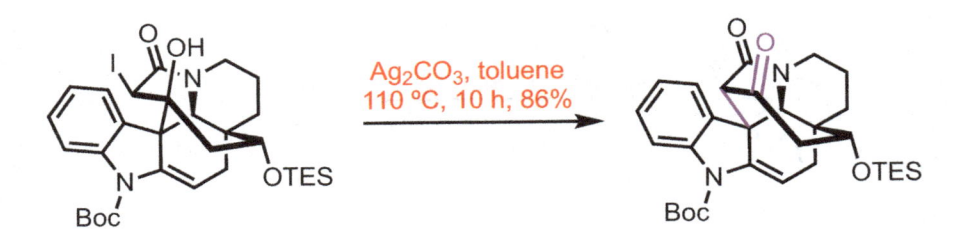

Ag$_2$CO$_3$, toluene
110 °C, 10 h, 86%

A	Overman Rearrangement
B	Favorskii Rearrangement
C	Hofmann Rearrangement
D	Pinacol Rearrangement

#40

POCl₃, DCM, 50 °C, 4 h
then NaBH₄, MeOH, 0 °C
(35%, overall yield)

A	Pomeranz–Fritsch Reaction
B	Pictet–Spengler Reaction
C	Vilsmeier-Haack Reaction
D	Bischler–Napieralski Reaction

#41

A	Negishi Coupling
B	Stille Coupling
C	Heck Coupling
D	Sonogashira Coupling

#42

A	Prins Reaction
B	Pinner Reaction
C	Van Leusen Reaction
D	Ritter Reaction

#43

A	Chugaev Elimination
B	Nicholas Reaction
C	Wolff–Kishner Reduction
D	Barton–McCombie Reaction

#44

PhI(*m*cba)₂, I₂
DCM, rt, 16 h, 67%

PhI(*m*cba)₂

A	Bischler–Napieralski Reaction
B	Hofmann Rearrangement
C	Hofmann Elimination
D	Hofmann–Löffler Cyclization

#45

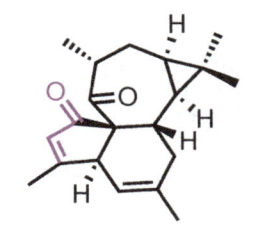

A	Rubottom Oxidation
B	Babler–Dauben Oxidation
C	Saegusa–Ito Oxidation
D	Baeyer–Villiger Oxidation

#46

A	Claisen Condensation
B	Baylis–Hillman Reaction
C	Michael Reaction
D	Aldol Reaction

#47

A	Vilsmeier–Haack Formylation
B	Gattermann–Koch Reaction
C	Bischler-Napieralski Reaction
D	Reimer–Tiemann Reaction

#48

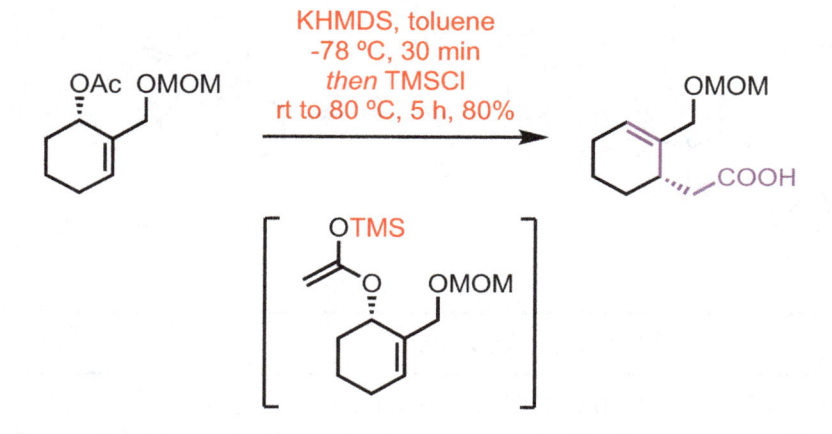

A	Claisen Rearrangement
B	Ireland–Claisen Rearrangement
C	Cope Rearrangement
D	Eschenmoser–Claisen Rearrangement

#49

Co$_2$(CO)$_8$
CO, mesitylene
rt to 160 °C, 26 h, 50%

A	Nicholas Reaction
B	Pauson–Khand Reaction
C	Schmidt Reaction
D	Diels–Alder Reaction

#50

A	Sonogashira Coupling
B	Arndt–Eistert Homologation
C	Corey–Fuchs Homologation
D	Seyferth–Gilbert Homologation

Named Reactions Handbook & Quiz

#51

Reagents: Hg(OAc)$_2$, AcOOH, AcOH, rt, 45 min, 55%

A	Mukaiyama Hydration
B	Baeyer–Villiger Oxidation
C	Fleming–Tamao Oxidation
D	Grieco Elimination

#52

A	Pinner Reaction
B	Overman Rearrangement
C	Claisen Rearrangement
D	Cope Rearrangement

#53

Reagents: Mn(acac)$_2$, PhSiH$_3$, O$_2$, EtOH, rt, 2.5 h, 81%

A	Mukaiyama Hydration
B	Fleming–Tamao Oxidation
C	Saegusa–Ito Oxidation
D	Babler–Dauben Oxidation

#54

A	Matteson Homologation
B	Corey–Fuchs Homologation
C	Horner–Wadsworth–Emmons Reaction
D	Seyferth–Gilbert Homologation

#55

A	Corey–Gilman–Ganem Oxidation
B	Pinnick Oxidation
C	Swern Oxidation
D	Rubottom Oxidation

#56

A	Criegee Oxidation
B	Baeyer–Villiger Oxidation
C	Dakin Reaction
D	Saegusa–Ito Oxidation

#57

A	Staudinger Reaction
B	Appel Reaction
C	Gabriel Synthesis
D	Delépine Reaction

#58

A	Beckmann Rearrangement
B	Curtius Rearrangement
C	Hofmann Rearrangement
D	Schmidt Reaction

#59

A	Claisen Condensation
B	Aldol Reaction
C	Dieckmann Condensation
D	Robinson Annulation

#60

A	Peterson Olefination
B	Takai Olefination
C	Wittig Olefination
D	Tebbe Olefination

#61

A	Aldol Reaction
B	Claisen Condensation
C	Michael Reaction
D	Dieckmann Condensation

#62

A	Birch Reduction
B	Noyori Assymetric Hydrogenation
C	Clemmensen Reduction
D	Staudinger Reaction

#63

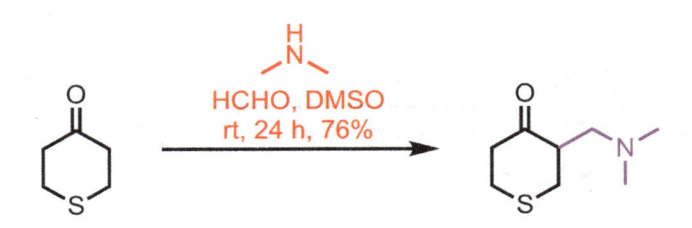

A	Claisen Condensation
B	Aldol Reaction
C	Mannich Reaction
D	Pictet-Spengler Reaction

#64

A	Wittig Olefination
B	Tebbe Olefination
C	Shapiro Olefination
D	Peterson Olefination

#65

A	Wittig Olefination
B	Horner–Wadsworth–Emmons Reaction
C	Julia–Kocienski Olefination
D	Corey–Winter Olefination

#66

A	Bischler–Napieralski Reaction
B	Mannich Reaction
C	Friedel–Crafts Reaction
D	Pictet–Spengler Reaction

#67

A	Stille Coupling
B	Negishi Coupling
C	Heck Coupling
D	Nozaki–Hiyama–Kishi Reaction

#68

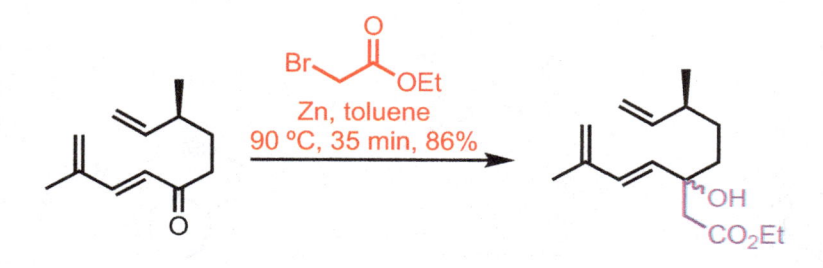

A	Strecker Condensation
B	Negishi Coupling
C	Reformatsky Reaction
D	Claisen Condensation

#69

(72%, *dr* = 5:1, 3 steps)

Reagents: 1. Co$_2$(CO)$_8$, DCM, rt, 1 h; 2. BF$_3$·Et$_2$O, rt, 3.5 h; 3. CAN, acetone, 0 °C to rt, 1 h

A	Pauson–Khand Reaction
B	Sonogashira Coupling
C	Sakurai Allylation
D	Nicholas Reaction

#70

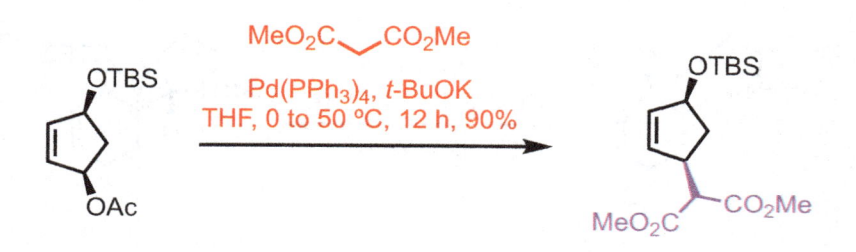

A	Tsuji–Trost Allylation
B	Sakurai Allylation
C	Mitsunobu Reaction
D	Appel Reaction

#71

A	Corey–Kim Oxidation
B	Ley–Griffith Oxidation
C	Parikh–Doering Oxidation
D	Swern Oxidation

#72

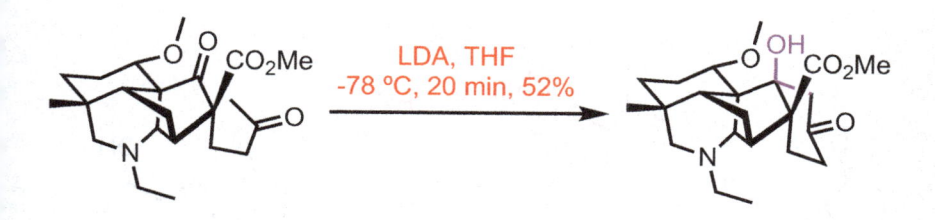

LDA, THF
-78 °C, 20 min, 52%

A	Claisen Condensation
B	Aldol Reaction
C	Dieckmann Condensation
D	Michael Reaction

#73

A	Sakurai Allylation
B	Roush Allylation
C	Tsuji–Trost Allylation
D	Suzuki Coupling

#74

A	Sonogashira Coupling
B	Stille Coupling
C	Heck Coupling
D	Chan–Lam Coupling

#75

ClTi(O*i*Pr)₃, EtMgBr
THF, 0 °C to rt, 36 h, 63%

A	Grignard Reaction
B	Barbier Coupling
C	Corey–Chaykovsky Cyclopropanation
D	Kulinkovich Reaction

#76

A	Nazarov Cyclization
B	Beckmann Rearrangement
C	Favorskii Rearrangement
D	Hofmann Rearrangement

#77

Catalyst
Oxone, K$_2$CO$_3$, MeCN
0 °C to rt, 3 h, 70%

(−)-Catalyst

A	Corey-Chaykovsky Epoxidation
B	Matteson Epoxidation
C	Shi Epoxidation
D	Sharpless Epoxidation

#78

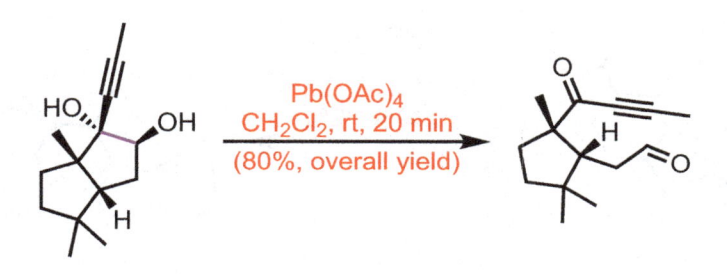

A	Baeyer-Villiger Oxidation
B	Pinnick Oxidation
C	Criegee Oxidation
D	Pinacol Rearrangement

#79

A	Aldol Reaction
B	Dieckmann Condensation
C	Michael Reaction
D	Henry Reaction

#80

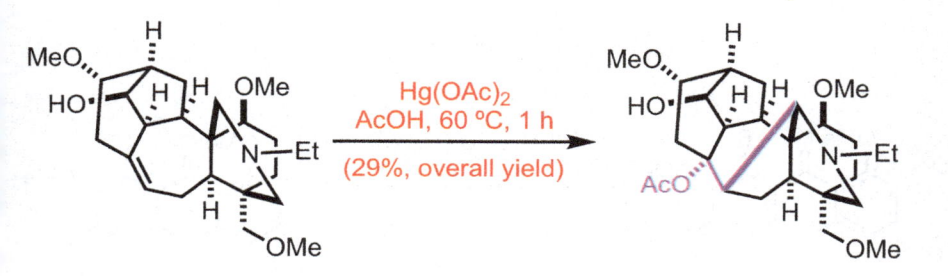

A	Prins Reaction
B	Pinner Reaction
C	Ritter Reaction
D	Mannich Reaction

#81

A	Chan–Lam Coupling
B	Ullmann Coupling
C	Buchwald–Hartwig Coupling
D	Suzuki Coupling

#82

NaClO₂, NaH₂PO₄
t-BuOH/H₂O, rt, 14 h, 71%

A	Pinnick Oxidation
B	Ley–Griffith Oxidation
C	Parikh–Doering Oxidation
D	Criegee Oxidation

#83

A	Horner–Wadsworth–Emmons Reaction
B	Julia–Kocienski Olefination
C	Still–Gennari Olefination
D	Wittig Olefination

#84

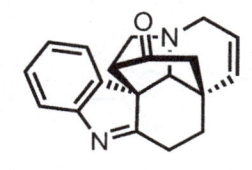

CH(CN)₂OAc
imidazole, MeOH
0 to 25 °C, 1 h, 88%

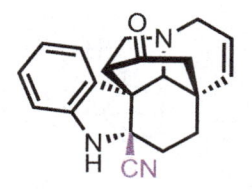

A	Gabriel Synthesis
B	Mannich Reaction
C	Petasis Reaction
D	Strecker Synthesis

#85

Reagents:
1. Phthalimide, PBu₃, DIAD, THF, rt, 1 h, 70%
2. N₂H₄, rt, 16 h, 51%

A	Delépine Reaction
B	Appel Reaction
C	Gabriel Synthesis
D	Staudinger Reaction

#86

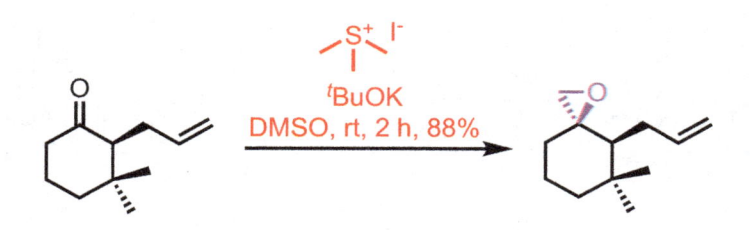

A	Matteson Epoxidation
B	Sharpless Epoxidation
C	Corey–Chaykovsky Epoxidation
D	Shi Epoxidation

#87

A	Cope Elimination
B	Grieco Elimination
C	Hofmann Elimination
D	Chugaev Elimination

#88

A	Bischler–Napieralski Reaction
B	Vilsmeier–Haack Formylation
C	Gattermann–Koch Reaction
D	Reimer-Tiemann Reaction

#89

A	Huisgen Cycloaddition
B	Diels–Alder Reaction
C	Ireland–Claisen Rearrangement
D	Eschenmoser–Claisen Rearrangement

#90

A	Suzuki Coupling
B	Miyaura Borylation
C	Matteson Homologation
D	Chan–Lam Coupling

#91

A	Horner–Wadsworth–Emmons Reaction
B	Wittig Olefination
C	Julia–Kocienski Olefination
D	Still–Gennari Olefination

#92

H₂, 1100 psi
RuCl₂[(R)-BINAP]
EtOH, 30 °C, 6 days, 76%

A	Corey–Bakshi–Shibata Reduction
B	Evans–Tishchenko Reaction
C	Noyori Asymmetric Hydrogenation
D	Staudinger Reaction

#93

A	Ireland–Claisen Rearrangement
B	Claisen Rearrangement
C	Cope Rearrangement
D	Eschenmoser–Claisen Rearrangement

#94

A	Suzuki Coupling
B	Heck Coupling
C	Sonogashira Coupling
D	Stille Coupling

#95

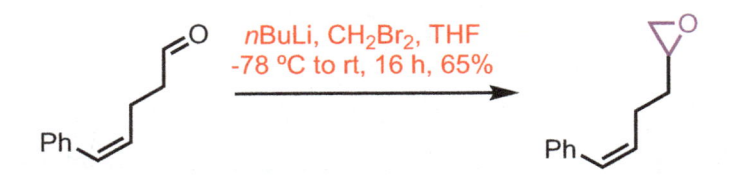

nBuLi, CH$_2$Br$_2$, THF
-78 °C to rt, 16 h, 65%

A	Shi Epoxidation
B	Sharpless Epoxidation
C	Matteson Epoxidation
D	Corey–Chaykovsky Epoxidation

#96

H₂SO₄, MeOH
reflux, 16 h, 45%

A	Claisen Condensation
B	Fischer Esterification
C	Yamaguchi Esterification
D	Steglich Esterification

#97

SnCl₄, DCM
0 °C to rt, 30 min, 75%

A	Diels–Alder Reaction
B	Nazarov Cyclization
C	Heck Coupling
D	Pauson–Khand Reaction

#98

A	Chugaev Elimination
B	Barton–McCombie Reaction
C	Peterson Olefination
D	Corey–Winter Olefination

#99

A	Noyori Hydrogenation
B	Evans–Tishchenko Reaction
C	Corey–Bakshi–Shibata Reduction
D	Van Leusen Reaction

#100

A	Mitsunobu Reaction
B	Appel Reaction
C	Hell–Volhard–Zelinsky Reaction
D	Haloform Reaction

#101

A	Suzuki Coupling
B	Negishi Coupling
C	Stille Coupling
D	Heck Coupling

Named Reactions Handbook & Quiz

#102

MeTi(O*i*Pr)$_3$, Et$_2$Zn
*i*PrOLi, LiI, 37%

A	Kulinkovich–Szymoniak Reaction
B	Simmons–Smith Reaction
C	Corey–Chaykovsky Cyclopropanation
D	Sharpless Reaction

Afterword

NROChemistry provides a range of resources to support your ongoing self-education efforts. Whether you prefer visual explanations, interactive quizzes, or in-depth mechanisms, there's something for everyone. With the following channels, you can continue mastering your knowledge and engage with a vibrant community of passionate chemists.

Youtube

On my YouTube channel, *Named Reactions in Organic Chemistry*, you'll find over 180 educational videos. These videos are thoughtfully designed to facilitate your study. The channel is constantly evolving, and new video concepts and ideas emerge. To expand the scope of the channel, I introduced new total synthesis videos showcasing real examples of well-known reactions. The videos about the synthesis of approved drugs allow you to explore the synthesis of the molecule, the mechanism of action of the drug, and its therapeutic target. With each video, you'll gain a deeper understanding of the crucial role named reactions play in the development of life-saving medications. The channel offers a comprehensive learning experience at your fingertips. From foundational reactions to cutting-edge applications.

Instagram

For bite-sized educational content, follow me on Instagram at *lluis_llorens_org_chem*. There, you'll discover over 200 educational posts, including raw footage videos of reactions being set up in a lab. Test your knowledge with quiz-type posts, delve into the intricacies of named reactions, and join a community of learners who share the same passion as you.

Website

To access a well-organized collection of named reactions, mechanisms, and examples, visit *nrochemistry.com*. The website provides free quizzes to verify your understanding of organic chemical reactions. Additionally, the Science Blog, part of the website's content, features the latest advances in organic and medicinal chemistry to keep you abreast of cutting-edge research.

My plans for the future

This book is only the beginning. Expect more volumes of the **Named Reactions Handbook & Quiz** in the future, each offering new reactions and examples. In 2024, I will be publishing **The Chemists' Cookbook**, a comprehensive guide that will teach you how to "cook" chemical reactions. It will cover everything you need to understand the reactions that chemists perform daily in their labs. If you don't want to miss out, subscribe to my newsletter, and I'll notify you as soon as it's available.

Thank you!

I want to take a moment to express my heartfelt gratitude to each and every one of you. Your support, engagement, and passion have transformed NROChemistry into a thriving community of intelligent chemists from all corners of the world. Every piece of content I've created is the result of a genuine desire to help passionate learners like you.

If you've found this book valuable, I kindly ask for your feedback. Please consider leaving a review on Amazon or sending me a direct message on social media. Your opinion will not only help me produce even higher-quality content but will also guide other chemistry students and researchers in discovering the value of NROChemistry.

Thank you for joining me on this journey. I look forward to continuing to explore the vast realm of organic chemistry together.

Lluís

List of correct answers from Part 2

#01 C	#21 B	#41 C
#02 B	#22 B	#42 D
#03 D	#23 C	#43 D
#04 D	#24 A	#44 D
#05 C	#25 A	#45 C
#06 A	#26 C	#46 B
#07 D	#27 B	#47 D
#08 C	#28 C	#48 B
#09 C	#29 C	#49 B
#10 A	#30 D	#50 C
#11 A	#31 C	#51 C
#12 C	#32 B	#52 B
#13 B	#33 C	#53 A
#14 B	#34 D	#54 D
#15 B	#35 B	#55 A
#16 A	#36 C	#56 B
#17 D	#37 B	#57 A
#18 B	#38 D	#58 C
#19 B	#39 D	#59 C
#20 B	#40 D	#60 B

#61 B	#75 D	#89 B
#62 A	#76 C	#90 C
#63 C	#77 C	
#64 D	#78 C	#91 D
#65 B	#79 C	#92 C
#66 D	#80 A	#93 D
#67 B		#94 D
#68 C	#81 C	#95 C
#69 D	#82 A	#96 B
#70 A	#83 B	#97 B
	#84 D	#98 D
#71 B	#85 C	#99 B
#72 B	#86 C	#100 D
#73 B	#87 C	#101 A
#74 A	#88 B	#102 A

About the Author

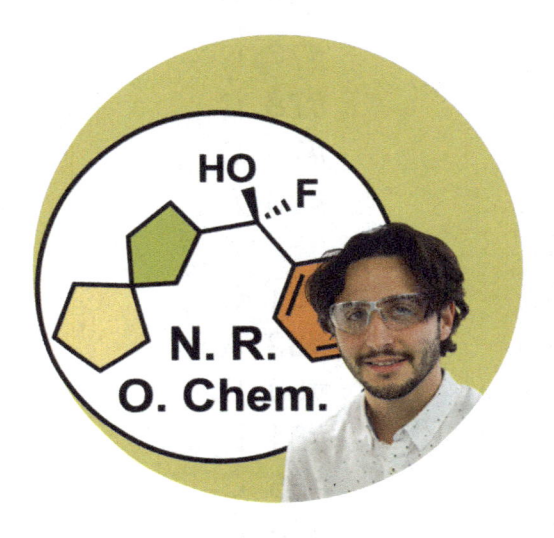

Lluís Llorens Palomo is an organic chemist who works on the optimization of leading structures in research projects. He is working on the design and synthesis of small molecule compounds in medicinal chemistry and integrated drug discovery campaigns. He is currently working as a senior scientist at Selvita, one of the largest preclinical contract research organizations in Europe. In 2019 he obtained his Ph.D. in chemistry at the Institute of Chemical Research of Catalonia, ICIQ, under the supervision of Prof. Dr. M. A. Pericàs. Since then, he has been producing online educational content about organic chemistry through his website, nrochemistry.com, and social media. The *Named Reactions Handbook & Quiz: Volume 1* is his first book from the NROChemistry series.

Connect with me

Email: lluis@nrochemistry.com

Website: www.nrochemistry.com

Youtube: Named Reactions in Organic Chemistry

Instagram: lluis_llorens_org_chem

LinkedIn: Lluís Llorens Palomo

Made in United States
Orlando, FL
14 February 2025